Mindwords

Unraveling the Psycholinguistics Maze

Freudian Trips

Copyright Page

Disclaimer

The views and opinions expressed in this book are those of the author(s) and do not necessarily reflect the official policy or position of any other agency, organization, employer, or company. The contents of this book are for informational and educational purposes only and are not intended to serve as professional advice, diagnosis, or treatment.

The information provided in this book is believed to be accurate and reliable as of the date of publication. However, it may include some errors or inaccuracies, and no warranty or guarantee is provided regarding the accuracy, timeliness, or applicability of the content.

Readers are encouraged to consult with professional philosophers, educators, or other qualified professionals where appropriate for personalized advice. The author(s) and publisher shall not be liable for any loss, damage, or harm caused or alleged to be caused, directly or indirectly, by the information or ideas contained, suggested, or referenced in this book.

By reading this book, the reader acknowledges and agrees that they are solely responsible for how they interpret and apply the information contained herein.

This book may also include references to other works, studies, and sources. These references are provided for further reading and exploration and do not imply endorsement or validation of the specific theories, viewpoints, or interpretations presented in those works.

Introduction: Exploring the World of Psycholinguistics

Defining Psycholinguistics: The Meeting Point of Mind and Language

Imagine you're at a bustling cafe, surrounded by the melody of human voices. Each word, each pause, each inflection is a part of a complex dance of communication. This is where psycholinguistics lives – at the crossroads where our minds process and produce language.

Psycholinguistics is like a detective. It seeks to unravel the mysteries of how we understand, produce, and use language. It's not just about words and grammar; it delves into how our brains turn thoughts into spoken or written words, and how these words are understood by others.

Think of a baby, absorbing the sounds and rhythms of speech long before they utter their first word. Psycholinguistics explores this journey – from the first "goo-goo, ga-ga" to the fluent speeches of adulthood. It's about understanding how language develops in our minds from infancy and how it shapes our thinking, identity, and relationships with others.

The Relevance of Psycholinguistics: Unraveling the Tapestry of Human Communication and Cognition

But why should we care about psycholinguistics? Because language is central to our existence. It's the tool we use to express our deepest feelings, share our thoughts, and connect with others. It's also a window into the human mind, offering insights into how we think, learn, and perceive the world.

For instance, have you ever wondered why some jokes are funny, or why certain words can stir powerful emotions? Or how about the challenges faced by someone learning a new language, or the struggles of someone with a speech disorder? Psycholinguistics helps answer these questions and more.

Moreover, understanding psycholinguistics is crucial in today's globalized world. As we interact with diverse cultures and languages, understanding the psychological aspects of language helps in bridging gaps and fostering better communication.

In essence, psycholinguistics is about understanding ourselves and others better through the lens of language. It's a journey into the human mind – a journey that helps us appreciate the power of words and the intricate ways they reflect and shape our thoughts, emotions, and social interactions.

In the chapters that follow, we'll dive deeper into this fascinating world, exploring how we learn languages, how our brains process and produce speech, and how language influences our thoughts and society. So, let's begin this journey into the captivating world of psycholinguistics, where every word is a clue to understanding the human mind.

Chapter I: The Building Blocks of Psycholinguistics

A Journey Through Time: The Evolution of Psycholinguistics

Let's embark on a time-traveling adventure to explore the evolution of psycholinguistics. Imagine psycholinguistics as a growing tree, with its roots deep in history and branches spreading into various fields of study.

Long ago, philosophers like Plato and Aristotle pondered over language and mind. Fast forward to the 19th century, when scholars began seriously studying how the brain and language interact. This was the seed from which psycholinguistics sprouted.

In the 20th century, the tree grew rapidly. B.F. Skinner suggested that we learn language through imitation and reinforcement – think of a child mimicking words and getting praised for it. But then, Noam Chomsky, a key figure in this field, shook the branches. He proposed that our ability to use language is innate – something we're born with, like a built-in software in our brains.

The late 20th and early 21st centuries saw the tree flourish with new branches. Researchers started exploring how culture, society, and individual differences affect language. The field of psycholinguistics had grown into a lush, vibrant tree, full of diverse ideas and perspectives.

The Puzzle Masters: Key Theories and Models

In this section, we'll meet some of the 'puzzle masters' of psycholinguistics – thinkers who have tried to piece together how language works in our minds.

After Chomsky's groundbreaking ideas, many others followed. Some focused on how we understand and produce sentences in real-time – a bit like how a skilled chef prepares a meal on the fly, using various ingredients (words) to create delicious sentences.

Others looked at language processing as a network of interconnected words and concepts, much like a spider web where each strand is connected to many others. This helps explain why hearing the word "apple" might make you think of "fruit," "red," or even "pie."

The Brain's Symphony: Understanding Language Neurologically

Our final stop is the brain – the orchestra conductor of language. Modern technology, like brain imaging, has allowed us to peek inside this complex organ while it processes language.

Different parts of the brain play different roles in language. There's Broca's area, involved in producing speech, and Wernicke's area, crucial for understanding language. Damage to these areas can lead to language difficulties, which has helped researchers understand their functions.

Moreover, we now know that language processing involves a symphony of brain areas working together. It's like a well-rehearsed orchestra where each section – strings, brass, woodwinds, and percussion – plays its part to create a harmonious melody.

As we close this chapter, we've seen how psycholinguistics has evolved, explored key theories and models, and peeked into the brain's role in language. This foundation sets the stage for understanding how we acquire, use, and are sometimes challenged by language. Just like a tree or a symphony, language is a dynamic, living thing that's integral to the human experience.

Chapter II: The Journey of Language: From Babble to Banter

Baby Talk: The First Steps in Language Acquisition

Imagine language as a magnificent castle. Each word is a brick, each rule of grammar is mortar, and infants are the master builders. From their first cry, babies are tuned into the language around them, absorbing sounds, rhythms, and patterns like little sponges.

In the first year, this journey begins with coos and babbles, like a musician practicing scales before playing a symphony. These sounds are universal – babies across the world babble in similar ways. It's their way of preparing the tools – their mouths and brains – for the complex task of speaking.

As they grow, babies start to recognize and imitate words. By their first birthday, many can say a few simple words like "mama" or "dada." This is when the foundation of the language castle starts taking shape, one word at a time.

But it's not just about speaking. Understanding comes first. Long before they can say words, infants understand them. They respond to their names, follow simple instructions, and react to familiar phrases. This shows that language is not just about talking; it's about connecting and communicating.

The Magic of Multilingualism: Learning More Than One Language

Now, imagine a child growing up in a house filled with two or more languages – a linguistic treasure chest. This is the world of bilingual and multilingual children.

Contrary to old myths, learning multiple languages doesn't confuse children. In fact, it's like a workout for the brain. It enhances mental flexibility, improves problem-solving skills, and can even delay the onset of age-related cognitive decline.

Bilingual children switch between languages effortlessly – a skill known as code-switching. This doesn't mean they're confused. Rather, they're adapting to their conversational context, much like choosing the right outfit for the right occasion.

Growing up with more than one language is like having a passport to multiple worlds. It enriches cultural understanding and opens doors to diverse ways of thinking.

Navigating Language Disorders: Challenges and Triumphs

Not everyone's journey with language is smooth. Some face obstacles like dyslexia, which makes reading a challenge, or aphasia, where language is impacted by brain injury. There are many other language disorders, each presenting its own set of hurdles.

Dyslexia, for example, is like trying to assemble a puzzle with pieces that constantly change shape. Words and letters might appear jumbled. But with the right support and strategies, many with dyslexia learn to read and write effectively, sometimes developing unique problem-solving skills along the way.

Aphasia, often resulting from a stroke or brain injury, can affect speaking, understanding, reading, or writing. It's like knowing what you want to say but finding the words locked in a chest. Recovery varies, but therapy can help rebuild language skills.

These disorders highlight the complexity of language and the resilience of those who navigate these challenges. Their journeys remind us that language is a gift, and it comes to each of us in different ways.

From the first coos of a baby to the multilingual conversations of a seasoned traveler, from the challenges of dyslexia to the recovery paths of aphasia, language is a journey. It's a fundamental part of being human, connecting us to each other and to the world. As we explore this journey further, we learn not just about language, but about the incredible adaptability and strength of the human spirit.

Chapter III: The Invisible Dance of Words: Understanding Language Processing

The Art of Conversation: Deciphering and Forming Speech

Imagine attending a concert where the orchestra is the human voice, and every conversation is a unique piece of music. This is the world of speech perception and production – the realm where we decode sounds into meaning and transform thoughts into spoken words.

When we listen to someone speak, our brains are like skilled detectives. They pick up sounds – the vowels and consonants – and swiftly piece them together into words and sentences. This happens so quickly and smoothly that we hardly notice the complex process underlying our understanding of spoken language.

But what about speaking? It's like painting a picture, but with words. Our brain first conjures up a thought, then finds the right words, and finally coordinates our mouth and vocal cords to articulate these words. It's a remarkable feat, considering how effortlessly we chat about the weather, share stories, or argue about politics.

The Gateway to Knowledge: Reading and Writing

Now, let's switch gears to reading and writing – the pillars of literacy. These skills are like keys that unlock the vast world of knowledge and imagination.

Reading begins with recognizing letters and associating them with sounds – a process known as decoding. Gradually, this decoding becomes fluent, and we start to extract meaning from strings of text. It's like solving a puzzle where each piece is a word, and the picture is the story or information being conveyed.

Writing, on the other hand, is like building a bridge. It connects our internal thoughts to the external world. It starts with an idea, which we then translate into words and sentences, organizing them in a way that makes sense and effectively communicates our message. Whether jotting down a grocery list or penning a novel, writing is a powerful tool for expression.

Memory: The Language Librarian

Our journey into language processing would be incomplete without discussing memory – the librarian of our language skills. Memory plays a crucial role in both understanding and producing language.

Short-term memory is like a temporary workspace. It holds onto words we just heard or read, allowing us to make sense of sentences and conversations. Think of it as a sticky note where we briefly jot down information before it either fades away or is stored more permanently.

Long-term memory, however, is like a vast library. It stores our knowledge of words, grammar, and all the nuances of language acquired over a lifetime. It's where we keep the meanings of words, the rules of grammar, and the templates for constructing sentences. When we speak or write, we pull from this extensive library to find the right words and phrases.

Understanding language processing is like watching an intricate dance of the mind. It's a dance that involves listening and speaking, reading and writing, remembering and forgetting. Each step, each move, is a testament to the incredible capabilities of the human brain. As we continue to explore and understand this dance, we gain not only insight into how language works but also a deeper appreciation for the power and beauty of human communication.

Chapter IV: Language: The Social Fabric of Our Lives

Sociolinguistics: The Colors of Speech in Society

Think of language as a chameleon, changing its colors based on the social environment. This is the essence of sociolinguistics – the study of how our language varies and adapts in different social contexts.

Every day, we switch between different styles of speech without even thinking about it. We talk differently to a child than we do to our boss, use different words with friends than with strangers. This isn't just about being polite or formal; it's about identity. The words we choose, the accents we have, even the slang we use, all tie us to our communities, regions, and social groups.

For example, think of a teenager using the latest slang with friends, then switching to a more standard language at a job interview. Or consider how accents can instantly tell us something about a person's background. Sociolinguistics explores these variations and what they tell us about social structures, relationships, and identities.

Pragmatics: Understanding Beyond Words

Pragmatics is like reading between the lines. It's the study of how context influences the meaning of language. It's not just about what we say, but how we say it, when, and to whom.

Imagine someone says, "It's cold in here," while sitting in a room. Are they simply stating a fact, or are they subtly asking someone to close a window or turn up the heat? That's pragmatics – understanding that the meaning of words can change depending on the situation, tone of voice, or even body language.

Context is king in pragmatics. The same words can mean different things in different situations. Understanding this helps us navigate social interactions more smoothly and avoid misunderstandings.

Language and Emotion: The Heart's Echo

Language is not just a tool for communication; it's also a powerful conveyor of emotions. Think about how a few kind words can lift your spirits, or how a harsh comment can ruin your day. This is the realm where language and emotion intertwine.

Our choice of words, the intensity of our tone, and even the pace of our speech can express a wide range of feelings – from joy and love to anger and sorrow. Poets and writers are masters of this, using language to evoke powerful emotions in their readers.

But it's not just in literature. Everyday conversations are laden with emotions. The language of emotion is universal, yet also deeply personal. Understanding this aspect of language gives us insight into human psychology and helps us empathize with others.

Language is more than just a system of communication. It's a mirror reflecting our social world, a tool for navigating the complexities of human interactions, and a bridge connecting our inner emotions with the outside world. By exploring sociolinguistics, pragmatics, and the emotional aspects of language, we gain a deeper understanding of not just language itself, but of humanity. As we continue to explore these facets, we enrich our understanding of the social tapestry that language weaves in our lives.

Chapter V: The Frontier of Language: Exploring New Horizons in Psycholinguistics

Neurolinguistic Programming (NLP): A Melding of Mind and Language

Imagine if you could reprogram your brain the way you update software on a computer. This idea is at the heart of Neurolinguistic Programming (NLP), a fascinating yet controversial concept at the crossroads of psychology and language.

NLP proposes that there's a connection between neurological processes, language, and behavioral patterns learned through experience. It suggests that by changing how we speak and think, we can impact our behavior and emotions. For example, NLP techniques might encourage you to visualize success and use positive language to overcome a fear of public speaking.

While NLP has its enthusiasts, it's important to note that it's seen as controversial and lacks substantial scientific backing. Critics argue that it oversimplifies the complexities of the human mind and language. Nevertheless, NLP remains popular in some self-help and corporate training circles, providing an interesting lens through which to view the power of language on thought and behavior.

Artificial Intelligence and Language: Deciphering Human Speech with Technology

Now, let's turn to a field where science fiction meets reality: the use of artificial intelligence (AI) in understanding and replicating human language. This is where computers are not just tools but participants in our language-rich world.

AI in language involves teaching computers to understand, interpret, and even produce human language. It's the technology behind voice assistants like Siri or Alexa, translation apps, and chatbots. These systems analyze vast amounts of language data to learn how to mimic human speech patterns, comprehend requests, and provide relevant responses.

The implications are enormous. AI could revolutionize how we interact with technology, breaking down language barriers and creating new ways of communication. However, it also raises questions about privacy, the nature of human interaction, and the limits of machines in replicating the nuances of human speech.

Future Directions: Where Language Meets Tomorrow

As we look to the future, psycholinguistics stands on the brink of exciting new discoveries and challenges. The field continues to evolve, driven by technological advances, new research, and changing societal needs.

One emerging area of interest is how digital communication – texting, social media, online forums – affects language and communication. Another is the growing understanding of how cultural differences impact language processing and use.

Additionally, there's a growing interest in applying psycholinguistics to real-world problems, such as improving education methods, refining language therapy techniques, and enhancing AI communication systems.

As we explore these frontiers, we're reminded that language is not static. It's a dynamic, ever-evolving entity that reflects and shapes our experiences, technologies, and societies.

In this chapter, we've glimpsed the cutting edge of psycholinguistics, from the controversial realms of NLP to the digital frontiers of AI in language. These advanced topics not only push the boundaries of our understanding but also open up exciting possibilities for the future. As we continue to explore these areas, we're reminded of the infinite complexities and capabilities of human language and the mind. The journey of psycholinguistics, much like language itself, is ever-evolving, filled with endless questions and possibilities waiting to be discovered.

Conclusion: The Unfolding Story of Psycholinguistics

The Ongoing Journey of Psycholinguistics: Exploring New Paths

As we come to the end of our exploration of psycholinguistics, it's clear that this field is not just a collection of theories and experiments. It's a living, evolving story – one that continues to unfold and reveal new mysteries and insights about how we use and understand language.

Like any journey, the path of psycholinguistics is filled with both challenges and possibilities. One challenge is the sheer complexity of language itself – a system that varies wildly across cultures and individuals. There's also the task of bridging the gap between theoretical research and practical application, ensuring that what we learn about language can benefit society.

But the possibilities are boundless. As we delve deeper into the workings of language and the brain, we stand to unlock new ways of learning, communicating, and even thinking. Each discovery opens doors to new questions, inviting us on a never-ending quest for understanding.

Implications for Education, Therapy, and Technology

The insights gained from psycholinguistics have profound implications in many areas, most notably in education, therapy, and technology.

In education, understanding how language develops and is processed can transform teaching methods. It can lead to more effective ways of teaching reading and writing, especially for those with learning difficulties. It can also inform strategies for teaching new languages, making education more accessible and inclusive.

In therapy, psycholinguistics offers tools for diagnosing and treating language disorders. By understanding how language processing can go awry, therapists can develop better intervention strategies for conditions like dyslexia, aphasia, and language delays. This knowledge can bring new hope and improved quality of life to individuals facing these challenges.

The field of technology, particularly AI and machine learning, also stands to benefit greatly. As we better understand human language processing, we can develop smarter, more intuitive AI systems. These systems could revolutionize how we interact with technology, making it more natural and user-friendly.

Looking Ahead: The Uncharted Territories of Language

As we close this chapter, it's exciting to think about what the future holds for psycholinguistics. New technologies, like brain imaging and machine learning, offer unprecedented ways to study language. Societal changes, like increased digital communication and multicultural interactions, provide new contexts for exploration.

The journey of psycholinguistics is far from over. It's a path that promises to enrich our understanding of one of the most fundamental aspects of being human – our ability to communicate through language. As we continue to navigate this fascinating landscape, we can look forward to new discoveries that will undoubtedly enhance our understanding of ourselves and the world around us.

Appendix: Pioneers and Innovators in the World of Psycholinguistics

In this appendix, we'll meet some of the key figures who have shaped the field of psycholinguistics. Think of them as the architects and builders of the vast, intricate structure that is our understanding of language and the mind.

1. Noam Chomsky: The Revolutionary Thinker

Noam Chomsky is often called the father of modern linguistics. In the 1950s and 1960s, he introduced the idea of "universal grammar," suggesting that the ability to learn language is hard-wired into our brains. Chomsky's theories shifted the focus from behaviorist views of language learning (which emphasized learning through imitation and reinforcement) to an innate capacity model. His work laid the groundwork for much of today's research in both linguistics and psycholinguistics.

2. B.F. Skinner: The Behaviorist Voice

B.F. Skinner, a leading figure in behaviorism, viewed language learning as a process of conditioning. According to Skinner, children learn language through imitation, reinforcement, and association. While his views were largely challenged and overshadowed by Chomsky's theories, Skinner's work remains influential in understanding the environmental aspects of language learning.

3. Steven Pinker: The Language Instinct Explorer

Steven Pinker is known for his work in the psychology of language and his book "The Language Instinct." He expanded on Chomsky's ideas, arguing that the human brain is naturally equipped for language learning. Pinker's work has been crucial in popularizing psycholinguistics and making complex ideas about language accessible to a broader audience.

4. Lev Vygotsky: The Social Interactionist

Lev Vygotsky, a Russian psychologist, emphasized the role of social interaction in language development. He proposed that language and thought are fundamentally linked and that children learn language through social activities. His theories highlight the importance of the social environment in the development of language and cognition.

5. Eleanor Rosch: The Categorization Specialist

Eleanor Rosch is known for her work on categorization and how language influences our thinking. Her research on how we classify and name colors, for example, has provided insights into the relationship between language and perception. Rosch's work helps us understand how the words we use shape the way we see and understand the world.

6. Elizabeth Bates: The Multifaceted Researcher

Elizabeth Bates made significant contributions in multiple areas of language development, including the acquisition of syntax, the relationship between language and other cognitive processes, and language disorders. Her work was notable for its interdisciplinary approach, combining insights from psychology, linguistics, and neuroscience.

These key figures, among many others, have paved the way for our current understanding of psycholinguistics. Their diverse approaches and theories provide a rich tapestry of insights into how language and the mind interact. As we continue to build on their foundational work, the field of psycholinguistics will undoubtedly continue to grow and evolve, offering new and deeper understandings of this fascinating aspect of human nature.

About Freudian Trips

Welcome to Freudian Trips, your dedicated platform for diving deep into the world of psychology. We are more than just a YouTube channel or a book publisher. We are a beacon of enlightenment, making complex psychological concepts accessible and engaging for all.

Our YouTube channel is a rich repository of psychology made simple. We take the profound and often complex ideas from the world of psychology and break them down into digestible, easy-to-understand content. From the foundational theories of Freud to the cognitive insights of Piaget, we cover a broad spectrum of psychological schools and thoughts, making psychology accessible to everyone, regardless of their background or prior knowledge.

As a book publisher, we take the same approach, transforming intricate psychological theories into comprehensible narratives. Our books are not just collections of words, but vessels of wisdom that make psychology approachable and relatable. We believe that psychology should not be confined to academic circles, but should be available to all who seek to understand the human mind and behavior.

At Freudian Trips, we believe in the power of curiosity and the pursuit of knowledge. We are here to stoke the fires of your curiosity, to guide you on your intellectual journey, and to help you navigate the fascinating world of psychology.

If you are someone who is not afraid to question, to explore, and to learn, then you are in the right place. Join us on this journey of exploration, as we make psychology easy to understand, one concept at a time.

Be sure to visit our Youtube channel at: www.freudiantrips.com/youtube

You can also visit us on the web at www.freudiantrips.com

Welcome to The Freudian Trip community. Stay curious. Stay enlightened.